Passover
Festivals Around the World

Words in **bold** can be found in the glossary on page 24.

©2016
Book Life
King's Lynn
Norfolk PE30 4LS

ISBN: 978-1-910512-96-8

Written by:
Grace Jones

Designed by:
Matt Rumbelow

A catalogue record for this book
is available from the British Library.

Passover

Festivals Around the World

When you see Jacob, he will tell you how to say a word.

What is a Festival?

A festival takes place when people come together to celebrate a special event or time of the year. Some festivals last for only one day and others

Some people celebrate festivals by having a party with their family and friends. Others celebrate by holding special events, performing dances or playing music.

What is Judaism?

Judaism is a **religion** that began around four thousand years ago in the Middle East. Jewish people believe in one God who they pray to in a **synagogue** or a Jewish place of **worship**.

A Synagogue in Prague.

The word rabbi means 'teacher' in Hebrew.

Jacob says:
SIN-A-GOG (Synagogue)
RAB-EYE (Rabbi)

Jewish people read a holy book called the Torah. The Torah sets out God's laws which instruct people on how to practise their **faith**. A **rabbi** teaches Jewish people about God's word through the Torah.

What is Passover?

Passover is a festival celebrated by Jewish people for seven or eight days in April every year.

Passover is also called 'Pesach'.

Jewish people come together to celebrate a time in history when they were freed from **slavery**. They celebrate by having a special meal, cleaning their houses and telling each other stories.

Jacob says:
PAY-SACK (Pesach)

The Story of Passover

A long, long time ago in Egypt, there was once a rich and powerful **Pharoah**. The Pharoah had many Jewish slaves, called **Israelites**. He treated them very unkindly. One day, a good-hearted man called Moses went to the Pharoah and asked him to free the Israelites. The Pharoah refused. Moses gave him a warning "If you do not free them, God will send terrible **plagues** to Egypt."

True to Moses' word, ten horrible plagues came to Egypt. One made painful boils appear on the skin of every Egyptian. Another sent millions of slimy frogs across the land.

Jacob says:
Go to page 22 to learn how to say these words.

God's final plague was to kill the eldest son in each house. Moses told the Israelites to mark their doors with Lamb's blood so God would **pass over** their houses. They did what Moses said and their sons were safe from harm.

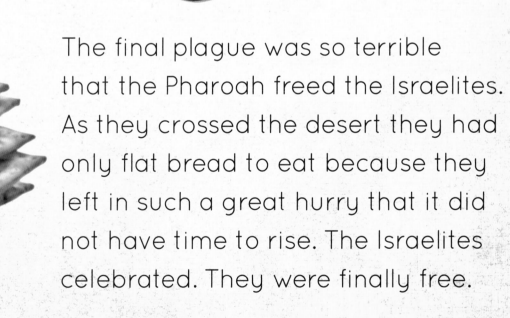

Pharoah

Flat Bread

The final plague was so terrible that the Pharoah freed the Israelites. As they crossed the desert they had only flat bread to eat because they left in such a great hurry that it did not have time to rise. The Israelites celebrated. They were finally free.

Festival of Freedom

Jewish people celebrate Passover to remember the time when God 'passed over' their houses and saved their eldest sons. This is why the festival is called Passover.

The world's largest Passover meal took place in Kathmandu, Nepal; more than one thousand people took part.

The festival also celebrates the Jewish peoples' faith in God and remembers a time in history when they became free.

Cleaning the House

Before Passover begins, Jewish people clean their houses. They search all over the house to get rid of any bread, cakes or biscuits.

Jewish people get rid of all leaven food, or food that has **yeast** in it. This is to remember the time when their people crossed the desert with only flat, unleavened bread to eat. If they find any, they put it in a bag and burn it.

Festive Food

On the first two nights of Passover, a special meal, called the **Seder** is eaten with family and friends. Unleavened bread, called **matzah**, is made to remember the time when the Israelites crossed the desert with only flat bread to eat.

Three Matzah are eaten at the Sedar meal.

Matzah

Bitter herbs, such as parsley, are eaten as part of the Seder meal. It is dipped in salt water to remember the tears of the Jewish people when they were slaves in Egypt. This part of meal is called the **karpas**.

Jacob says:
SEE-DER (Seder)
MAT-ZA (Matzah)
CAR-PAS (Karpas)

A traditional karpas eaten at Passover.

Parsley

Salt Water

The Seder

During the Seder meal, people read aloud from a Jewish book, called the Haggadah. The book tells of the story of how the Jewish people escaped the Pharoah and Egypt.

Jacob says:
HAG-A-DA (Haggadah)
MAG-ID (Magid)

The youngest child at the table then asks their father four questions about the Seder. After the father finishes giving the answers, a cup of wine is drunk.

The asking of questions at Passover is called the Magid.

Family and Games

During the Passover meal, three matzah are put on the Seder plate. A piece of the middle and biggest matzah is hidden somewhere in the house. The person who finds it wins a prize and shares it with their family.

Although Jewish people celebrate their faith in God during the festival, Passover is also about spending time with family, friends and loved ones.

Jacob Says...

HAGGADAH
HAG-A-DA

A book about the story of how the Jewish people escaped Egypt.

ISRAELITES
IS-RAIL-ITES

Jewish people born in Africa.

KARPAS
CAR-PASS

A part of the Seder meal where bitter herbs are eaten.

Magid
MAG-ID

The asking of four questions at the Seder

Matzah
MAT-ZA

Unleavened bread eaten at the Seder meal.

Pesach
PAY-SACK
The name Jewish people call Passover.

Pharoah
FAIR-OH
A great king of Egypt.

Rabbi
RAB-EYE
A teacher of the Jewish faith.

Seder
SEE-DER
A Jewish feast that takes place during Passover.

Synagogue
SIN-A-GOG
A synagogue is a Jewish place of worship.

Glossary

Faith: Great trust in someone or something.

Plagues: a disease or a large number of animals causing harm.

Rabbi: a Jewish teacher of the Torah.

Religion: a set of beliefs based around a god(s).

Slavery: people who are not free.

Worship: a religious act, such as praying.

Yeast: the ingredient that makes bread rise.

Index

Credits

Photocredits: Abbreviations: l-left, r-right, b-bottom, t-top, c-centre, m-middle. All images are courtesy of Shutterstock.com. Front Cover: bg – Maglara; l – SergiyN; r – Noam Armonn. 2 - Maglara. 4 - Tom Wang, 5 - Noam Armonn. 6 - DeepGreen. 7 - Anneka. 8 - Maglara, 10 - Matej Kastelic, 11: tr – mountainpix; bl - maratr. 12 - Borya Galperin. 13 - aastock. 14 - grafnata. 15 - Sea Wave. 16 - tomertu. 17 - R. Roth. 18 - Sunny studio. 19 - Noam Armonn. 20 - maratr. 21 - Golden Pixels LLC. 22/23 - Marco Govel.